W9-BBH-609

PENGUIN POETS

WHO SHALL KNOW THEM?

Faye Kicknosway is a freelance writer and artist who
has published seven poetry collections with small presses;
her drawings have been included in juried and invi-
tational shows. In 1985 she was awarded a National
Endowment grant for poetry.

ALSO BY FAYE KICKNOSWAY

O. You Can Walk on the Sky? Good.
Poem Tree
A Man Is a Hook. Trouble.
The Cat Approaches
Nothing Wakes Her
Asparagus, Asparagus, Ah Sweet Asparagus
She Wears Him Fancy in Her Night Braid

FAYE KICKNOSWAY

Who Shall Know Them?

PENGUIN BOOKS

PENGUIN BOOKS
Viking Penguin Inc., 40 West 23rd Street,
New York, New York 10010, U.S.A.
Penguin Books Ltd, Harmondsworth,
Middlesex, England
Penguin Books Australia Ltd, Ringwood,
Victoria, Australia
Penguin Books Canada Limited, 2801 John Street,
Markham, Ontario, Canada L3R 1B4
Penguin Books (N.Z.) Ltd, 182–190 Wairau Road,
Auckland 10, New Zealand

First published in simultaneous hardcover and paperback editions by
Viking and Penguin Books 1985

Published simultaneously in Canada

The completion of this book was made possible by an Individual Artist Grant from the Michigan
Council for the Arts.

LIBRARY OF CONGRESS CATALOGING IN PUBLICATION DATA
Kicknosway, Faye.
    Who shall know them?
    I. Title.
PS3561.I32W5   1985   ·   811'.54   84-27682
ISBN 0 14 042.345 1

Acknowledgment is made to the following publications in which some of the poems in this book
originally appeared: *Barnwood*, "I Was Dragged Down"; *Hanging Loose*, "Someone Is Always
Dying."; *Invisible City*, "Look at Her:" (under the title "Violence"); *Ironwood*, "The House in
This Picture," (under the title "The Violence of Potatoes"); *Moving Out*, "Kitchen" (in different
form); *New Letters*, "Portrait"; *Nimrod, Ontario Press Review*, and *The Generation of 2000
Contemporary American Poets*, "The Horse."

Line drawing by the author.

Printed in the United States of America
by R.R. Donnelley & Sons Company, Harrisonburg, Virginia
Set in Bodoni Book

For my friends
from whom
without whom

Author's Note

The characters in these poems are imagined from the photos of Walker Evans, but they have nothing to do with the real lives of the actual people. I am particularly indebted to Walker Evans's photograph "Bud Field and His Family, Hale County, Alabama, Summer 1936," which he took for the Farm Security Administration collection now in the Library of Congress. I find the photograph deeply moving and the figures in it are not static to me, but vulnerable and alive.

Contents

Who Shall Know Them?

I Don't Know Her

This woman here, sloppy-shouldered,
squint-eyed, I don't know her.
Nor this room
she's in. Those wooden walls
and floors. All stained-up.
All whopper-jawed
and needing nails and paint.
I don't know her.

The size
of her nose or her mouth
pulled up. The sleeping kid
she holds.
I couldn't name you her

if you asked me. Nor him,
nor the rest of them all lined out
and held so still. Unnatural.
I've seen fish
on a string
down a country boy's back
look more natural
than they look, posed close
together, not scratching, not
with the window opened and the old
one there, looking out.

And his handkerchief's not knotted
tight
on his neck like he usually wears it.

And her, with the safety pin,
the young
one, getting long-boned and moony,
scratching her toes
against the wood, I don't know her,
neither.
Nor do I care to.
That suspicious old lady,
head cocked, sideways looking out
at me, new shoelaces in her shoes,
I wouldn't look out
my window
to look at her, nor listen
to her talking
at the vegetables
in her backyard garden.

None of them is worth the time
and they've all
been dead
longer years than I been born
and living.
And the road out front
don't lead no where near their house, it
sitting in the hollow
down lower than that stand
of trees out back
of the chicken coop.

And that little picture tacked
on the wall back there

where the old man can see it
but the kids have to stand
on the wash tub turned over,
don't mean a thing to me.

And the shirt
over the door, you can see its
collar here, I've never seen it
on anyone
or anyplace other than right
there, it's always been just like that,
partly visible, at the top
of the picture.

But mostly her,
it's mostly her
I don't know. I maybe seen
pictures of rooms
like this, and kids
sleeping or awake—all tilt-faced
and dreamy-eyed
like that one, or wanting to run
by the side
of the house with the dog,
throwing sticks

and giggling, like that little one
there
held in between his father's knees—
I maybe seen

kids like that, running in the street
or in the alley.

Even that old lady, I've seen her
too, or someone like her,
peeking around a curtain, the room
behind her
dark and never opened. And him,

he's everywhere; I see him
any time of the day.
But her,
I've never seen her.
That big hand rolled into a fist,
those feet bent double
under her,
that little edge of slip
showing underneath her checker dress; no,

I've never seen her before
nor do I care to see her now.
Her hair
all knotted
and black, those bug bites

showing on her chest
where her dress is opened.
The dirt on her and how she's all
slopped down
on the edge of the bed looking like
she hasn't any sense at all
behind her face.
I don't know her nor
do I care to.

She leaves that baby whining
on the floor
while she goes off in the field
looking for men.
She leaves it between chairs
so it can't crawl too far.
Everyday
she leaves it. She goes farther
and farther, sometimes

disappears in the weeds,
sometimes stands in the shade
of the trees looking out
at the men and rubbing her hand
on her arm
or scratching at the ticks
on her legs. She squints

under her hand and sometimes follows
the road, wagons coming along,

sometimes cars. She lies herself down
under a tree

and everything stalls
right there.
She's slower and slower
getting back. One day you'll take this

picture out to show me, to have me
story it for you, and there'll be
an empty place at the corner
of the bed. And the baby

will be all knotted up
and asleep on the sheet
with no momma anywhere near it.
She'll be gone,
she'll have disappeared down the road
so far
there'll be no time to call her back
so you can show me this

picture with her in it.
She'll be in the shade
of a tree or in the shade
of some man's arms.
And none of them
will see it, they'll all

be right there, lined up, looking straight
ahead and never sideways to see
if she's made it back in time.
She'll be gone,

and nobody will notice. The bed
will be ditched in from having
her weight on it in that spot
for so long, and the baby
will be asleep.
Nobody will notice.

You'll show me this picture
and I'll say, "Look at how

funny that bed looks, like someone's
been sitting on it."
And there won't be any way for me
to tell you about her;
she'll be gone.

And I could meet her on the street
and she could hello me
until her throat
got dusty, I wouldn't hear her.
You got to know
someone before you can hear them.
Before you can answer back.
And I don't know her.

Someone Is Always Dying.

Families are too big.
You could spend all
your time
going to funerals. There are two
brothers. They were on the bus
since before dawn; now,
they have to walk.
It's their father
who's died.

As they walk down the road,
they come upon a little valley.
Neither one of them seems
to remember it, and they stop

to look at how
the heat
rises from it.
I don't know their names; one of them
doesn't want to be here,
not even for his father's
funeral. He thinks his father
died on purpose
just to drag him back. Looking

down at the fields and trees
he thinks of his father's hands,
remembers their pressure,
their heat. That old man

died on purpose. His brother
doesn't feel it; he's tired,
hungry, he hasn't slept much and his clothes
don't fit well. His pants

are all twisted
and his shirt sticks to him.
He squats on his hams, smoking.

The first brother, who is older,
stands beside him,
his knees
locked, his hat pushed forward
over his eyes.
"I'd rather be dead
at the bottom of a sink hole
than waste my life
following a mule's ass
across a field."

The younger brother pushes
his smoke
from the tips of his fingers.
Stands.

Their little sister looks down
the road from the shadows
of the front porch at the car

driving crazy, hitting both edges
of the road.

She is thin
and tense and steps back
toward the front wall of the house
as the car stops and a man

climbs out.
She twists her wedding ring,
watches
the car disappear down the dirt
road. He looks up
toward the porch, grins as she

steps to its edge
into the sunlight.

And He Did Not Know Her,

although
he held his arms out
toward her, conjuring
that her embrace would give him sons
and a prosperous life.

She had walked toward him,
and her teeth,
and the cords in her neck,
and the posture
of her head above her stiff
shoulders should have been a warning
to him: he did not heed it.

What she seemed to be,
she was not: soft and fertile,
fleshy
as the heated banks of a river;

she was not even smoke
or ashes that are left
from a fire.

He had tricked himself,
seeded her
with his longing,
believing

that wherever
he set up house with her,

the air
would be humid
and the earth
green.

She had given him daughters,
painful to his eyes,
brittle, with tiny mouths
that bit moisture
from the air
leaving it more parched

than it had been.

Her dress
had moved softly
against him, but her eyes
had been beryl and malachite.
She was a thickness, a roughness
his hands were injured
touching.

He Has Been Threshed Out.

If you poked your finger
into him, it would come out
barely dusty.

The shade doesn't cool him;
he makes it itch.

His back is against the side
of the house
and his knees are up,
his hands rested upon them.

He scratches his chin,
fiddles
at the edge of his boot,
lifting his fingers

to his lips
to blow on them
like they've been singed.
If he took his boots off
and set them in the road,

the heat
would melt them.
The land is barren,
not even stones
grow from it.

If he leaned down
above it
and squeezed the sweat
from his fingers
onto it, the sweat
would rise
as steam

and blister the skin
of his face and hands.

Each piece of air
he sucks in
is like cinders
from a fire.

But he would rather
tie himself to the ants
in the road, or let his heart
fill with bracken

than enter
the house, its wallpaper
a flat, bright garden,
and her in it,

talking to the furniture,
scolding
or flattering it
as she pushes it from one part

of the room
to another.

It is her pleasure;

and he imagines her
stooping above
an overstuffed chair
and it rising up
on its two back feet
to dance with her.

It has teeth
in its underside
and they grind sideways
the way an animal eats.

His thoughts feel chewed through,
and he can not recognize them
as his
or understand them.

Trapped inside her body
is the soil
and climate he desires.
He knows it,

because her shadow is like
rainwater and it brings
to life

whatever thing in the house
it touches. It is spongy,

thick; the curtains,
lamps
and dishes are nested down
beneath it.

She has only
to stretch her hands
above a vase
or a basin
and cracks mend
and edges soften.

Sometimes, on purpose,
in the night, he wakes up.
Everything is still.
He listens
to her breathing,

turns toward her,
pretends to scoop up water
from her bare skin
into his cupped hands,
touching his fingers
to his face, surprised
at how cool
they are.

Linoleum

The floor
had been done up with linoleum,
but it was so scuffed
she tacked a rug
down
over it
to hide it,

and the rug bunched up
and she had to straighten it
each time
she moved a chair.

He remembered
the linoleum, how slick
and cool it was, the pattern
worn off, made slippery
and silvery
as freshets and streams
in sunlight.

He would slide
his bare toes along the marks
and grooves
in the linoleum, thinking
he would surely
scoop out tiny fish, at least
a panful.

With the pressure
of his toes,
he'd work at closing off
a stream,
diverting it
to pass under a chair
where he imagined
it would be shady

and cool
and lazier fish
would fatten.
He could feel

the linoleum
under the rug, but did not like
to, for the rug was always
caught up in ridges
when she vacuumed it,
and it was bumpy

under his bare feet, and its texture
was dry
and coarse.

The Horse

He'd rent the horse and it sounding like it had asthma
and its legs shivery
and its back dropped so far your feet dragged
on the ground when you sat on it
even if you was the youngest,

he'd rent it,
touching it on its side all the way down to its tail
and back up to its neck,
picking its feet up, squinting into its face,
prying open its mouth: horse,

it was after all
a horse
and all he needed was what it was
harnessed to the plough for a couple of afternoons,
he had a hand cultivator but it was hard,
slow work; that horse,

I always waited for it to die the way it shook
and wheezed,
and he'd hit it with the harness straps
and swear at it and say he could surely do it faster,
and it would pull and rattle at the harness
and he'd have his sleeves rolled up
and be hauling back on the plough,
pulling against the horse, and the ploughshares
would dig
into the dirt

and get stuck, and he'd have the harness wrapped
around him and in his hands as well as the plough

handles, his feet braced and his legs stiff,
his hat pulled deep on his forehead,
cussing his luck for having thought to do it
this way when he had good strong kids
could pull better, the horse too old

and sick to care, and him sweatier, and finally
so mad he wasn't mad at all,
his lips tight and disappeared right off
his face and his arms lumpy with his veins
all knotted out in his skin
and his shoes unlaced and full of dirt,

him more buried and turned over than the earth,
stiff-legged and measuring nothing with his eyes
like he had done when he began,
not looking
at where the sun stood in the sky and how long

it would take to do this much and then
that much and by mid-afternoon,
if he was lucky, maybe this part here
and that would leave over there and back behind that
little U in the trees to do.
Nothing. His eyes

straight ahead and on the horse's backside,
blinking the sweat loose sometimes
but mostly letting it settle and roll down
his eyes, not looking anywhere,
turning the horse around,
pulling on the plough, loosening it,
holding onto the animal and turning it all
around
to walk back up again, dipping the ploughshares
and pushing them
so that they were into the ground
and could claw it up
and out and him

as tired by the time she made him quit
as the horse had been when he had started,
giving him water and looking at him suspicious
and cautious of his mood
and what she could do to make it better
so he wouldn't be mad supper was late
when we got home, and him saying

if that horse died
on his land, the man who owned it
had better come and clear it off
and pay him back his money
and money besides for the time lost
looking at his goddamn dead horse,

whatever possessed him to think he needed
to use it, anyway.

He'd say it as he untied the harness straps
from around his back and arms and hands,
looking down at it like he hadn't never seen it
before and didn't know maybe
it belonged on trees
or should be thrown in the water
or used in the house somehow in the winter
near the stove, it so heavy and useless,
he spoke

so flat and low with no heat in his voice,
it all burned out of him by the sun
and the work he'd done and have to do again
tomorrow and probably, by the looks of it,
the next day, too,

and he'd heard there were better ways to live,
better ways, with only looking at the fields
from automobile windows as you drove
along beside them
and pointed out the window
and wondered what that hillbilly was doing,
and he was tired
of being the hillbilly
and tired
of being tied to this useless hide

of dog food all the days of his life,
and to this small patch of land—
worthless was what it was—
and he'd drink

from the dipper and us crowded together
back where he couldn't reach us with the harness straps
if he should try, looking
at him and at her, knowing she'd handle it,
she'd even out his temper before we took the horse
back and headed for home ourselves.

And as we went back
and it darkening
his mood toward the horse
changed
and he wasn't so sour toward it, it did the best
it could, old and lame
and sick as it was. The air

was cooler
and his body and legs weren't so knotted up
nor his arms,
his sleeves rolled down, his hat
pushed back on his head, the day
didn't hurt so much thinking about it
as we walked in the slow dark
toward home.

Kitchen

My mother, when
she was young and first married,
I did not see her there, but I imagine her
by the stove.
My father, in the room nearby, wakes.
She hears the noise

of his body moving on the bed.
He is exhausted, even before he rises,
and he scrapes his thick fingers
through his hair and looks
beyond the doorway of the room
in which he lies
toward the lighted room where she is.

She pulls plates down from the shelf,
puts them on the table;
he hears the hiss
of bacon frying, smells the coffee.
His life feels perfect;

he stands, pulls his clothes from the hook,
looks into the dark, thinking
she is beautiful, there is no need
for any other
in his life.

He moves from the dark toward her,
slips his hands down her dress;
she scolds him; he cups his hands.

"Go wash yourself." The water
fills the basin, spills
from it.
He shudders in the cool
dark, straightens.
The morning smells of dust,
of cobwebs and burned wood.

Soon the sun will lift
above the trees; he will be gone
into the heat
of the factory.
He eats quickly, watching her.
He stands. She does not move
as he moves
toward her.

The sun makes a sound
in the morning—silver—rattling clear
as pump water.
Dust rises slowly, is brittle
and wheel-like.

She feels fingers come alive out
of the wood of the tables,
the walls; they catch
at her skirt, at the skin
of her legs and arms.

She brushes past them, feels
the dust move
slowly
and perfectly; in time,

if she stood still long enough,
it would cover her.

Dust is in her nose
and eyes.
Flies nest in her hair, her collar;
she feels their little hands.

The clock ticks.
Noise comes into the room
through the window. The sun

makes a high-pitched sound that is like
the sound her nerves make;
she feels it behind her eyes,
and her skin
is alert
and flinches
at the touch of the air
against it.

Portrait

There was mud in her;
she was like a field
animal
and nothing moved her.

Whether she sat
or stood, she dawdled
or dreamed.
There was no
pleasure, nothing

that rose up
full
from within her.

She yawned,
her jaw hung open,
she stared into space,
her fleshy cheeks hanging
below her eyes
like the back-end
of bloomers.

If she smiled at all,
it was vague;
if she looked at you at all,
it was a surprise
like being bumped into.

She said
nothing, loomed up
like a sow

come from its pen
to an unfamiliar place.
She filled

the doorway
and no light
could come through it,

or breeze.

He Went Out, Dust

rising around him with each step.
The heat
made him shiver. It picked
at his hat
and his knees. There was no moisture
in the air
or in the earth
or in his body.

Death;
It was surely Death, and the sun
was Its agent killing everything
except the choke weeds
and scrub that gave nourishment
to nothing, digging

with long, claw-like roots deep
into the earth,
siphoning water up
from so far down
he could not
dig them out.

Her flesh; water leaped out
of her
and fell back into
her. Dress pulled up,
its hem bunched in her fingers,
she sat on the porch,
fanning her thighs.

Although the fields were her life
as well as his,
she did not look upon it
that way: to her,
they were his only and he
would be damned.

His pride
that stood him up bawling
how strong he was, and how he could
wrest whatever he wanted
from the land, his swaggering

and shifting of his arms in the air,
his assurance
that he had a deeper strength
than the earth
and the plants that grew
from it
had damned him.

The dry air, the blistered ground,
the weeds
that stole so easily
whatever moisture there was
from the sickly plants
he had tried to fasten into
the earth
were his rightful
harvest.

Of that she was certain, and she sat
in her conceit
watching him labor in the field
believing
that the dust
which rose up
and fell down around him
was his own flesh.

How she had longed to pin him down,
to take his noise away from him
and fill his mouth
with silence.

And she sat
in the heat, corpulent
and rubbery, too greedy
for the sight of him in his defeat
to go inside the house
and sit
where it might be cooler.

The House in This Picture,

I built it.
It was cardboard and unpainted. No rain;
only shelter.
I knew who it was and climbed its skirts;
gentle, so gentle.
I travelled it soft, dreaming.
Its skirts sang meat, and
its silences. It spat and spat, its heart
toothless.
I'm lunatic.
This one here, this little one,
thing:
no pleasure.
I can't read this, it's a picture; here, you take it,
you read it.
Take it.
They lie bunched against their
dreams, everything alive, out of focus.
I breathe them.
I'm tired. Sweaty and thirsty. These children,
their metal eyes,
this picture, the odor of porches
turned solid.
I'm tired. Tired.
No food. My window is boarded closed.
But I hear
her flesh; it jumps at me.
It jumps.

There is a noise like trains in the dark.
Dogs whine. She is soft, in miniature, her coarse

thick hair.
I see her everywhere,
on the heels of shoes,
her blue eyes. So large
and her lips. I'm not safe; this picture;
look at her.
The ceiling. She ducks her head. So narrow,
full of anger.

Who Is She?

Look at how she sits.
That old man, is he her husband?
He's so scrawny-necked,
so dried up.

I bet she blows her nose
with her fingers, leans
one of her arms around a child,
bent forward a little,
her other hand at her nose;
her snot dries faster than she
can blow.
Maybe sometimes she uses
the hem of her dress

and the snot cakes there,
and her children
grab hold of her
and hug her with their faces
pushed into her dress.

Her face is crooked. It went
crooked in the sheet
or in his arms.
It got squashed up against him
one night, and it never
went back straight
again.

Look at how tired she is; it's as plain
as her hair
or her shoulders. Look at how
she shrugs forward.

Her mother is dead; and another thing,
she might be that old man's wife now,
but she was first
his daughter.

That old husband-man,
the sun has fiddled its way
through the holes in his hat
and has scorched
his brains.

She wishes she was dead
instead of her mother.
She used to follow her
down the bean rows, trying to touch
her dress.

And they'd go into town
together. Her mother would look in
at the dinette window.

Men would look up,
push back from their food,

wiping their lips
with their sleeves.

She's so tired; look at how thin
she is. Only her hair is fat.
It's getting darker
all around; she's smaller than
a midget.
I'll be the size of her,
but I'll be wrinkled up.
She'll catch me by my arm,

and this picture
will be lying
on an ironing board
and where she sat
will be empty; she'll have scraped
herself free and she'll force me
to sit there,
where she was,
and she'll iron me down,
making me flat
so that I fit.

I'll be alive,
and my hands will hurt,
and my head will be ditched down
into my shoulders.

The man who took this picture
thought his mouth had disappeared.
In its place was a hole
that might as well have spiders
or mice living inside it.
He thought that if he spoke
he'd make a noise like bushes
scraping against the side
of the house, or like flies
worrying
at the sunlight
on a porch.

He hadn't meant to bother with anyone.
He had his camera
on a string
around his neck, the husband put his hand
on the porch rail, she

was stooped forward in her chair,
shucking peas, the child
tied to her
in her apron.
She had looked up, pursed
her lips, squinted
her eyes.

He had thought only the sky
saw him, and that only the insects

jumping into the air
around him knew
he was there.

But they had watched him,
their faces already flat
and grey·
in the film
he had not yet wound
into his camera.

The River

I was young then, at the yard's rim,
sway-backed, belly poked forward,
my dress sash loosely tied,
the bow drooped and lopsided.
The bright yellow dust,
scratched loose
from the yard and the road, sifted up
my nose
and fattened out
my hair.

I stood splay-footed, toes
dug down into my shoes, elbows bent,
fingers in sweaty bundles, with my back
to the yard
which had no green to it, was merely
footpaths meandering up
from the drainage ditch
toward the house squatted down
beside its two sickly trees.

I was dizzy with sun, but did not take
myself to my favorite place
beneath the front porch
where I could sit crushed together, my chin
on my knees, spying out
at the yard or listening
to the noises in the house

travelling out from it
through the boards above me.

Across the road was a field, weed-packed,
brittle and high, full of grasshoppers
and flies that leaped
and scratched at my face and knees,
dropping down my collar or into
my shoes when I walked there. The weeds

had little fists of burrs
hung out from them and razor teeth
along their stalks that cut
my arms and legs or bit
into my hair, pulling it.

Beyond the field,
where I did not go,
was a dark, uneven line of trees.
It was hotter there,
and lying down beneath the trees
and covered over
by their branches
was the river.

The air was thick as spit;
the river breathed pieces of its water
up into it. If that air
came into my nose

and slid down my throat
to my lungs, they'd thicken
closed
and when I breathed
my ribs would break
and I'd sink down
to the ground.

The river was a hole
and the water covering it
was a trick. Under
the weeds near its banks
it pretended to be covered over.
There were edges of light
cast off from the waves
in the water that could blind me
even if I kept my eyes closed.

And once I was blind
the river had me
and would steal me
into its mouth
and chew me until I broke
into pieces.

That had happened
to my uncle
and my cousin, and my father

once sat fishing
in a boat
and the river pressed hard
against the boat, breaking it
and pulling it
under.

The sunlight white-knotted
in my hair, I stood
in the bald
and rusted yard.

The road
and the field beyond it
were green
and full of tiny flowers that felt
soft as plush
when I stepped on them.
I was taller than the trees
growing on the banks
of the river. They were like
pumpkin vines
around my legs and I leaned down
above them, pushing their leaves
aside. The river
glittered
like crushed glass
against my calves

as I stood straddle-legged
above it.
It lifted up
and fell back down
beneath me.

How beautiful it was.
How old.

My mother stepped down
from the porch
and entered the sunlight,
walking toward the edge of the yard
where I stood.
Her skirt hem was caught up
at her waist and her stockings
were rolled down to her shoe tops.

Her hair
was wet and as she walked
she bent forward, raising
her hands to it,
shaking it
and twisting it until
it seemed to glide
and boil.

"The sun cooks the earth
and cooks your brains, too,
if you stand in it

and gawk too long
at nothing," she said.

Her hair rippled and shone;
she combed her fingers through it,
parting it,
and I saw
dark, wavy spots between its strands
that were children
playing
up the road.

"The sun can addle you,
can make your brains
as bleached as laundry,"
she said, and she cast her hair

out into the air and it was both
net
and water. I squatted down
on my heels at her feet, letting it
touch me.

"Get away," she said, scraping
her fingers through it,
"Get away," but I hissed
and gabbled
around her feet
and she could not push me,
or shake me free.

The Grey Field

I set the plates
on the table.
Everything was at a boil.
He stepped to the kitchen
doorway;

I had the silverware
in my hand
about to lay it out
where it belonged.

"She said for me
to come up there."
He didn't move
from the doorway, the toes
of his shoes were rested
on the linoleum, his heels
on the rug.

"Now?" I asked him
putting the last fork
in its place.

"Yes."

I looked
at the table; it was set
just right.
The water glasses and the plates

were each above the bunches
of daisies in the oil cloth
that were still bright enough
to see, and all

that really showed of them
was the ribbon
that went around between them.

"Should I come up there
with you?"

He reached his hat down
from its peg.
"No," he said. "It's best
that you stay here."

"Does she mean
to stay there long?
Will she come home?"

"I don't know. You eat
your supper; I'll have mine
when I get back."

The door closed.
I walked around the table,
straightened napkins, knives,

the water glass
at the head
of each plate.
The sugar bowl. Salt shaker.

It was perfect;
there was no color to it.

River Hill Café

He was two days late;
his feeling had changed.
He said, "I'm thinking of too many things
right now."
He said, "I've caught you;
you can't flap your arms
and fly away."

They were at supper. Flies were all
around the meat
and he kept his hand out,
waving them away.
"Goddamn flies," he said.
The juke box was on, people
were slopping money
out of their pockets.
"It's different now," he said.
"Different."

She had to look at him, how
he was changing it all around.
They were purple in the light,
"violet" he called it.
She kept looking at her hand to see
the color better.
"I have to ease up," he said.
"I don't want a house with you;
I'm nervous about this.

I don't trust you; I'm away too
long."

She looked at him; he was already
gone. "It makes me depressed,"
he said. They had lain in the shade
so thick no sunshine could come

through it, and there were butterflies
all yellow and white
in the field,
the noise of flies and faraway
voices calling
and singing, and her skirt

was up and her legs
around him, and in her eyes
were the colors of cornflowers
and white daisies, day lilies
and goldenrod, and the ground

where she lay
was cushiony
and fit her back. How cool he is,
telling her, "I'm away
too much."

She had met him so quick; he had picked up
her bundle, grinned at her.

"I'll have tah scrub you with a Brillo
and clean you with a garden
hose," is what he had said to her.

And he made her
stand by his car
until he'd spread rags on the seat
for her to sit on.

Even her feet
had a rag from the trunk
and she had to be

careful she kept them on it.
He wiped his pecker off
with his handkerchief before he zipped his
pants while she stood there
all sticky on her thighs.
"Fuckin a hillbilly broad by the side
of the road, I just might catch
something from being so
stupid."

He'd be lying
on the couch, blinking his eyes
and scratching the hair
on his belly, and she'd be sitting
beside him, wanting to talk.
It was all so different.

"I'm tired; I don't need your noise."
She felt so feeble; her mouth
all flattened out.

And those cockroaches, when
they'd climb on him, he'd yell and beat
his skin where they had been
and he'd shake and be mad
and hit her. Like she had something to do
with them being in the room.
He'd tear the bed apart and move
it farther off
from the wall. There were cans of spray
everywhere and the air
was never fit to breathe, he chased
after them and sprayed them so solid
they were lathery.

She'd kiss him, she didn't know better,
it was all

so different from where she'd come from:
it was wallpaper
on the wall and a wash sink in the corner
and a little kitchen place near it.
He would touch on her so hard
and awkward she'd hurt.
"Do you love me?"
She couldn't answer. It was all she could
do sometimes not

to laugh at how ugly he was.
But the sheets were nice
and when she scrubbed underneath the ice
box
and inside the stove, the roaches
weren't so bad. And he got more peaceful
with her. She was always
uneasy with him. His fat belly
and his ass rolled out around him.

"Yes," she'd answer, first thinking
of the new dress he'd bought her
or the stockings. "I love you."
There was a rug
to stand on, her feet weren't cold
in the morning. She had curlers for her hair.
And nightgowns.
And underpants and brassieres
she couldn't count.
She'd rub her hand on the folds
in his belly skin, lower her head
and kiss the sweaty hair around his
belly button. "Lower," he'd say. "Kiss
me lower."

He never spent the night, didn't
come around much.
She'd cook him dinner.

He'd take his pants off. He'd stand
there or sit down or lie down and she'd
do it. His hands on his hips or his arms
crossed behind his head.

She had a looking glass long enough
she could see from her head
to her shoes.
There were stuffed chairs you'd sit back
in, comfortable.
He'd move his hips
and close his eyes, his lips partly opened.
"I'll give you a ride," he had said to her.
And she'd been sitting
by the side of the road
for so long.

Nobody but farmers
came by in their wagons.
And she wouldn't let them,
not anymore. She closed her skirt
and gathered up
her legs
when they climbed down

from their wagons and walked
toward her.
"What's the matter? You on the rag?"

"Yes," she said.
"Too bad," they said, all hot

and lathery, reaching down
her dress, swatting her
on her bottom.
"Too bad."

Billboards and Frame Houses

They went to the picture show together.
Her hanging onto him by his hand
and a little back. She felt awkward
in those shoes, and the stockings
made her legs sweat.
She was sweaty all over and had stuck
a handkerchief up her sleeve.
It made him laugh, seeing it.

"Put it in your pocket book," he said.
"But wonder if I need it quick,"
she answered. "Take it out,
silly," he said right back.
As though it would be that easy. Maybe

for one of those women walking comfortable
in her shoes, cool
and fragrant, with not so much scent
on she smelled like a drawer.
That's what he said to her. "Whew,"
he said. "Somebody close
that drawer."

And it was her, smelling
extra good for him right after
she had washed and scrubbed herself
all over.

"Wash it off," he said.
"Don't smell yourself up
so much that you stink."
She didn't stink; it was called *Lavender Mist*
and it had cost her over a dollar
at the dime store.
"Soap smells better,"

he said. "Maybe we can air
you out; let's walk a little."
But she tilted in her shoes
and her ankles wobbled. She had a ribbon
in her hair
and it curled
and her lips were red
as in the picture show.

"Take that grease off your mouth," he said,
and he stood contrary
in the doorway
until she had washed her face
pale again.

The Crossroads

He rented the mule,
saving out
a portion of his weekly wages
for that purpose, not

to walk behind it
or touch its harness
or even to take the reins up
into his hands
from where they lay
braided together
above the mule's collar,
he rented it

to sit on it, both his legs
dangled off
the mule's right side, his body
slouched forward,
his hands
rested
on his thighs.

He planned it, where he
and the mule would be,
by studying maps
after supper,
smoothing them flat
with his hands
as he leaned above

the kitchen table,
pencilling over the routes

between towns, measuring
how far it was between them
with a small, yellow ruler.

Because I was the youngest,
he'd usually let me watch.
My mother did not like me there,
so close to him, and if she could,
she'd send me off,

to fetch her a cloth
from beneath the sink, or thread
from its spindle
in her sewing box.

"Just mind your nose, Missy,"
she'd say to me.
"Let the child be," my father
would say and look at me
and grin.

I stood beside him, asked him
how to say the name
of a town, had he been there yet,
was it all built up
with houses like where we

lived, or was it mostly
fields.

I'd peek to see where she was
and tap his hand
where it lay against the map
and whisper:
"Can I come with you
when you get it?
Can I ride it, too?"

She always heard
and came at me,
cuffing me away
from the table.

"Why don't you stop
this foolishness?"
she'd say to him.
"I won't be party to it
anymore."

"You will," he'd answer her,
and stand up, tapping the map
with his finger. "Here

is where you'll see me."

He went alone
to get it, usually leaving

before first light
of a Saturday, her half-asleep,
glad to be rid of him,
watching out
the kitchen window
as the car backed down
the driveway.

She'd keep us in
and we'd all but hide from her
she'd be so sour.
He'd call her
on the telephone
to say how far

he'd gone and which bus
to take.

We'd be scrubbed up,
standing near the wash sink
by the back door,
kicking at the screen
or riling up the dog
by whistling to him
and slapping our thighs
like we would play with him.

We'd eat, then help her
make up a basket so we'd have

something
for later.

It was a day
out, and the first few times
it happened I hardly breathed
or sat. My older sister,

from the start, did not
like it and although she shared
what my mother felt,
she could not say it out
to her or come too close
to her with her own
grim face.

"What's into you, Missy?"
Mother'd ask her
staring hard enough at her face
to char it
and have it fall to ashes
down her collar.

"You wash those dishes
and keep a hand
on that temper
before I put mine
on it," she'd say,

and my sister would turn mute,
facing the sink
to do as she was told.

I itched
to go outside,
feeling that it was somehow
unnatural to be so tidy
on a Saturday. If any of my friends

came calling, they'd look at me
like I must be going
to a funeral
and she'd tell them
to go off,
I couldn't play.

My hair was washed
and even my shoes were cleaned;
I'd had to stand
at the edge of the back porch
with a stick

scraping the mud
from their soles and heels.

She'd mind the clock
and when it was time
to go, we'd each

have to come before her
so that she could be sure
we were fit
to go out.

We'd take turns ,
carrying the basket
down the road
to the bus station.
The child
who was obliged

to carry it, had to hold
it up tight
to the chest.

The bus station was part
of a store. There was a bench
along its outside wall
and she'd have us sit
along it while she went inside
to get the tickets.

They knew us after awhile;
at first, I'm certain
they puzzled over us,
wondering why

a man would let his wife
and children go off

without him
on a bus
of a Saturday.

She would not
allow us to go into
the store. She feared
we might blunder up
against the counters
or what was stacked
in the aisle,

knocking things down,
or we might be so taken
with what we saw,
we'd whine
and fret at her
to buy it.

If it was raining,
we'd come from home
clustered up against her,
sheltered under a large,
flowered oil cloth.

It hung down
behind us, bumping
against the backs

of our legs and shoes
as we walked,
splashing mud up
onto our white
stockings.

She'd leave us
under the oil cloth
while she went in
to buy the tickets.

I'd hear: "But, Missus,
you're surely welcome
to step inside," or, "Missus,

mightn't it be better
for the children
if they was to wait
inside?"

The screen door would open,
close, the oil cloth lift
as she took its edge back
into her hands.

Even in good weather
the waiting was awkward
and long, and I sat

on the bench, fidgety,
distracted
until the bus came.

My sister shared a seat
with me, and she squeezed
herself up
against the arm rest,
complaining that I
should be made
to sit still.

I was always
the first
to see him.

He'd be at the edge
of a field
near the crossroads.
The bus would stop.

If the mule
had acted up,
he would not
have known what
to do. I think the farmer
he rented it from
gave it a remedy

to make it stand still
while he sat
on it.

My sister
would look at him,
then drop her chin down
onto her chest
and fix her gaze
on the metal leg
of the seat
ahead of us.

My mother would look,
keeping her head turned
to the window
even after
the bus had started up again
and all
there was to see
was open fields.

When the bus reached
the next town, we'd get off
and set the basket down
on the bench

that stood along
the outside wall

of the bus station.
She'd tuck a napkin up
under our chins
and we'd eat.

"Someday that mule
will act up
and try to throw him
or turn
its head
and try to bite him,"
she'd say, "but I

won't be there
to see it, to have
some stranger poke me
in my ribs
and point at him
and say, 'Look at that jackass

of a farmer,
falling off
his mule.' "

What town it was
where she left us, I don't
remember, but she hadn't
scolded us
about our manners,

or polished at us
with her handkerchief
and comb, or kept us
close to her
as we walked.

There was a dimestore;
she said
we could go in.

By the time
we missed her,
she was gone
and there was nothing
that could be done.

Look at Her:

if you grab her, her skin'll be rough
on your fingers. She's the afternoon
moon, big and shadowy, she's the plough
or the tractor
or the chain fence, and she gets sticky
when you squeeze her.
She's the little silver zipper in his pants,
but she doesn't mind

and touches the freckles on her shoulder.
She doesn't mind
the size she is
nor that her eyes get red and her hands wet
when she touches them.
She sits at the edge of her bed, crosses
her arms above her sleeping child,
leans forward, her shoulders raised.
She squints.

Her fingers are onions
and other roots pulled from the ground.
She crosses her feet, thinks of him
asleep beside her.
She has thick hair and dark eyes.
She wishes he was less wrinkled and evil
smelling. In the night, she turns him young;
he walks toward her, she sits up,
holds her arms out.
His wiry fingers pinch her. She sits quieter

and quieter, undresses the hooks
in the closet. She does not dream,
nor does the wood around her,
nor do I,

asleep or awake. I hear doors open
and sweaty fingers
slide into apron pockets.
Her smell is urine, dried and crusted,
the inside hair
of her legs.
He drags himself closer, yawns and stretches.
I wander the bent floor minding the next meal
and the garden picked raw
by strangers.

And them, her family, opposite,
in a row, never moving, like a fruit-seller's
vegetables.
They are less than buttons,
less than little trays
of food handed around to the sick.
They are less than socks, folded up.
She is less than all of them,
less than him
and what he carries
in his morning pocket.

She has wanted to dream him.
And her mother stood

with water and newspapers.
He rubs his feet in the dirt,
back and forth, before he enters.
She lights the fire,
cuts things up, remembers dreams
of swimming, of fish

nibbling the hair on her legs.
They are to have their picture taken.
They are to sit together in a line.
Or stand, if the man directs.
The floor is at an angle, and they might
fall off.
He clears his throat, turning and plumping her
in his mind.
She is violet and silken; her smile distracts
him.

It is empty where he takes them, where he stands
them up. She picks her teeth with a thread
from her dress; he feels undone:
they giggle and punch one another in the arms
when he's done and ask
to see it.

My thoughts are beyond the river.
I look at where it's cool
and well-lighted. Where it's quiet.
The building squats behind me.

I sleep in the daylight, wake, dream
I'm drifting on the river,
one hand in the cold, green water.
I glance towards shore and see
them
brought out from their house,
made to stand.
I hear the oars move in the water.
There is a movement of cloth
at my shoulder.

Her Name

I can not name to you
what is present in this room,
or who sat where,
the names of the wood it took
to make the walls and floors,
to make the broom handles,
the mop handles, the square-shaped
box stuffed behind the kitchen stove,
the wood

it took to make the chairs
or the porch
under them, the pickets
of the fence down by the road,
or the loose

lumber stacked and scattered out
in back like it might be there
because someone had a plan to build
something with it.

Oak, maple, cedar
I know as words
and not as trees or what is made
from trees.

I might as soon be standing
down near the river
in the shade of a sycamore tree,

or of a cottonwood or an elder,
and I might notice that the leaves

have different shapes
and the trees stand forking
into branches some close down
their trunks, some higher up,

and that the shade from some trees
is thinner than the shade
from others, the wind

pushing the branches
so that the leaves
separate
and bright holes of light
come through; it is
easy

to see how trees are different.
And the planting of some too near
the water is dangerous to it,
because the trees will drink
the water up
and turn the land
dry; I know this,

but I can not tell you which
tree it is.

Or how wood is seasoned, how long
it takes or what is used
to season it, if it must be soaked
in brine
or in water or set out
in the sun
or stored
in the dark, or how the bark
is stripped from it, what tools
are used, whether it must be dried
before it's milled, the sap
let out of it from holes dug into
it, I can not tell you this,
or which wood

is best for which thing, the planking
of a house, its beams, or the fittings
inside it
when the house
is finished, or how the wood

in a rocking chair is bent,
or how the wood in a table
or a floor
is planed so that it is
straight.

I can not tell you which tree bark,
when the tree is young, is smooth
to the touch, but as it ages, it

ruptures and roughens so that your hand
touching it
is embedded with its texture
and with pieces
of its flesh.

I can not tell you how the leaves
turn color or when, which tree dies
with a yellow leaf
and which dies with a red.
I can not tell you how deep
the leaves get
beneath each tree, or how
to gather them and use them as cover
for smaller plants during winter.

I know wood must be dry
to burn, but which wood burns
slowly, I do not know.

What has been cut
and shaped from wood
holds heat. I know if a wooden bowl
is left on a counter
near a window
where the sunlight can touch it, it

will stay warm a long
time after
the sun has gone down.

I do not know why,
but if you touched
the bowl,

or picked it up,
holding it in your hands,
your hands
would be warmed
by it.

I Come In

from the dark
into the smell
of kerosene
and bedclothes.

The room
is empty;
there is newspaper
spread on the floor
beneath a window,
there is a table
pushed back
against the wall
with two kitchen chairs
tight
against it, their seats
and legs
buried in the dark

underneath it.
I come in
feeling a pressure
of people around me
and see no one.

I stand in the doorway,
the doorframe around me
like I was a picture
hung
from a wall. I come in

awkward, not knowing
what to do, should I
just stand there
or move away
to one side, should I
come directly
into the center of the room,

or should I enter it
slowly, keeping close
to the wall. I look around.

The room
is well-lighted,
but there are no lamps,
no bulb hanging
by its wire
from the ceiling, no candles,
no fire

in the fireplace.
I come in, squinting
against the light,
wanting to call out
but afraid to.

The room is warm.
Bare. A fine dust,
like that shaken

from a rug
or a blanket, moves
in the air.
I come in,

scuffing my feet
on the doorsill,
expecting to see
my sister, her dress loose
and her hair
in knots, bent

at the cookstove,
her hand
at the fire, the skillet.
There is kindling set
in the box. Her large
straw fan and her hat
hang from a peg
near the broom.

Where is she?
And my brothers?
Why aren't they
nested down
by the stove
licking molasses
from their fingers?
And my father,

why isn't he squatted down
near the wall, his hat
on the floor near his feet?

And my mother,
where is she, where
is the bed upon which she sat,
her bare feet rested
on their sides
on the floor,

her body bent forward
at the waist, her dark
eyes narrowed
and her gaze intent?

I Was Dragged Down

from my room at the top of the house one year when the wind
threatened. Momma had heard about it first on the radio and
had turned it off, and all the lights off, and would have torn the
telephone from the wall, thinking the wind and electricity would
be attracted to us down the wires, but Father would not let her.
I was dragged down and in my father's arms and I was small
enough not to understand the noise I heard nor the smell of fear,
my mother's voice sounding harsh and angry as she coaxed at
my sister to be calm—at me, although I was rolled up like a
little cat against my father's sweaty shirt.

Things broke free from the house, clattering against it. I slept
tucked into my father's arms, his chest noisy against my ear. I
woke up sometimes and saw my sister sitting in a chair near
Mother, the both of them stiff as my sister's dolls. Their hands
were held in fists between them, and their eyes were open so
wide I saw the whites clearly even in the dark.

The room we were in smelled wet and I could not remember it,
it was so changed by the light. The chairs rose and fell, they
were thicker than I remembered them and they burst and opened
and seemed to bend from stalks that began under the floor of
the house. The tables glowed, their polished faces bright as the
edges of flowers.

"O Momma, we'll be killed," my sister cried, and as I looked
at her, the light seemed to break her face into pieces.

I took that image of her into my sleep, and cradled in my father's arms I dreamed she walked out into the rushes and weeds near the river, and was taken slowly by the black water, first to the knees, her arms held out stiffly in the air, then to her waist, her white dress floating around her like it was growing up from the water and she had entered it, the meaty, large petals of a flower. It was like a bell or a globe; she hung at its center, and I watched the petals lift up and close around her. I cried out for her to come back, but the flower sank into the river. I made a net of my hair and cast it into the water, dragging against its weight. A dark thing, woven of sticks and mud and leaves, rose up and pulled at the net, drawing me into the water. I awoke, believing that it held me. My father tried to comfort me, alarmed at how afraid I was.